THE TREE

Written by Smriti Prasadam-Halls

Illustrated by Victor Tavares

Once there was a tree as old as the earth
and as tall as tomorrow.

No one could remember a time before the tree,
for its roots ran deep into the heart of the village.

It knew the people there and the people knew it.

The tree was a playground ...

a refuge ...

a sanctuary ...

and a home.

It was a tree of knowledge and of memory.

The capricious seasons came and went, blowing this way and that, but the tree stood faithful and firm.

Through summer's sultry breezes …

and autumn's golden glow

Through the icy chill of winter ...

till spring buds blossomed once more.

7

A little girl, as strong as sunshine and as young as yesterday, played in the branches of the tree.

She climbed its boughs …

She read in its shade …

She sheltered in its embrace.

The tree kept her secrets; it listened to her stories old and new.

And the tree watched as the girl grew up: curious, kind and courageous.

As the girl grew, so the small village began to grow.

Slowly at first and then faster and faster until there were many new friends to meet ... though none so true as her tall tree.

Homes were built. And buildings.
And the village became busier.
Soon, plans were underway to build
a big market for the whole village.
But to make room for the market …
the tree would have to go.

The girl clung to the branches in denial;
in defiance. It could not be so. It would not be so.
She studied the pictures and plans and projects.

And then she
protested …

She pleaded …

She persisted …

13

Days, weeks, went by, but no one seemed to hear her.
The louder she shouted, the quieter her voice …

until at last there was only silence.

Then, one day, the mechanical birds clanked in,
their motors humming an unwanted song.

The girl bid farewell to her tree.
She had tried her hardest to rescue it,
but it hadn't been enough.

The girl thought her heart would break.
Tenderly, she wrapped her arms around
the tree one last time and murmured goodbye.

Exhausted, she fell asleep.

That night a wild wind blew and the sky
flashed white but the girl knew nothing of it.

She slept long and she dreamed deep.

When she awoke the next day the air was new …

Bees buzzed. Squirrels scampered. The birds were singing.

And the market was open …

20

A market where children played and babies laughed; where people met and greeted one another beneath the beautiful sky ...

all held together by a tree.

A tree that knew the secrets, the dreams, the life and the loves of the families around it.

A family tree.

Once there was a girl as strong as sunshine
and as young as yesterday.

And there was a tree. As old as the earth …
and as tall as tomorrow.

A tree of knowledge, a tree of memory, a tree of HOPE.